Mary Jane's

HASH BROWNIES, HOT POT, AND OTHER MARIJUANA MUNCHIES

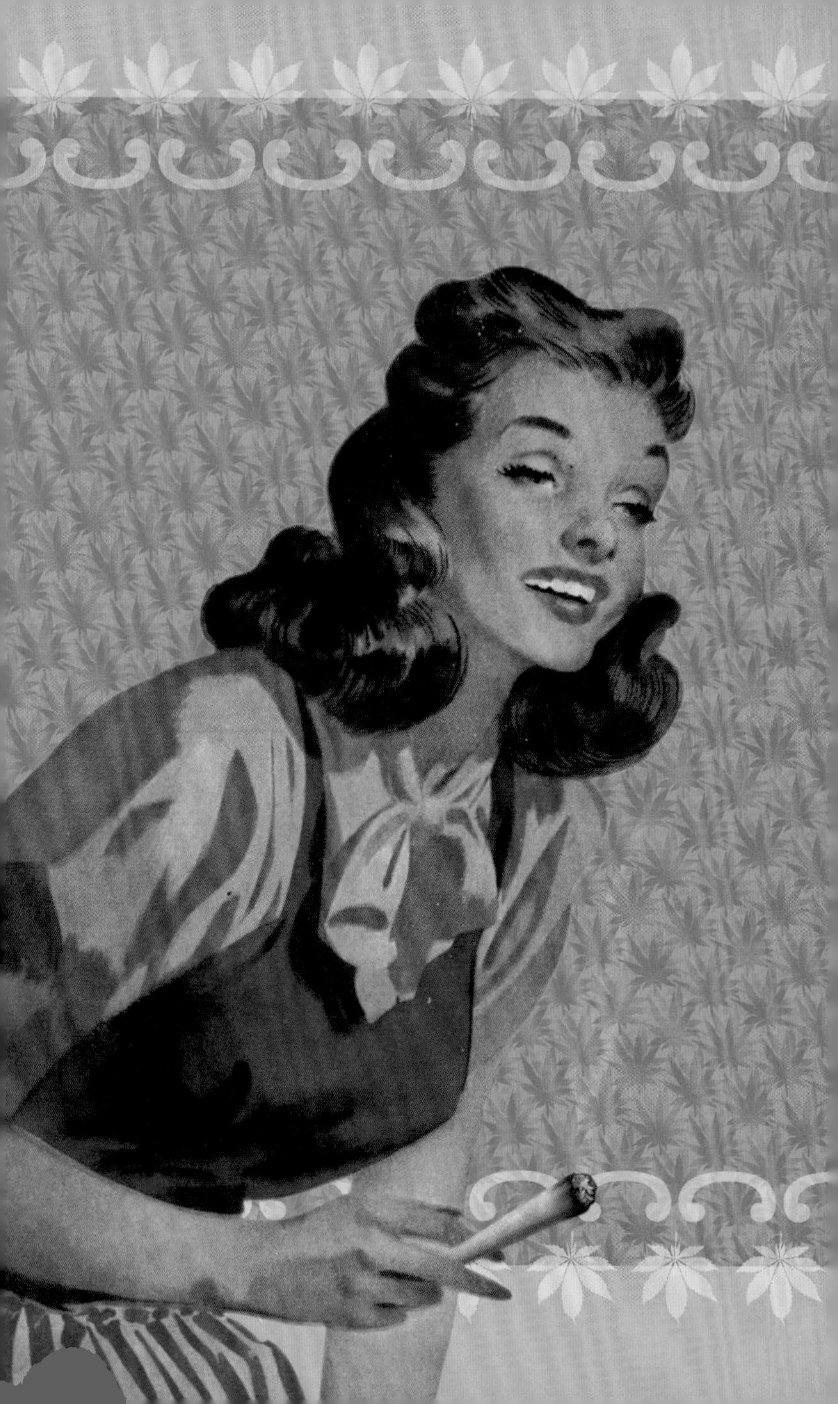

Mary Jane's

HASH BROWNIES, HOT POT, AND OTHER MARIJUANA MUNCHIES

30 delectable ways with weed

DR HASH

DOG 'n' BONE

This edition published in 2016 by Dog 'n' Bone Books
An imprint of Ryland Peters & Small Ltd

20–21 Jockey's Fields   341 E 116th St
London WC1R 4BW   New York, NY 10029

www.rylandpeters.com

Previously published in 2010 by Cico Books and in 2012 by Dog 'n' Bone Books.

10 9 8

A CIP catalog record for this book is available from the Library of Congress
and the British Library.

ISBN 978 1 911026 06 8

Printed in China

Editor: Catherine Osborne
Designer: Paul Tilby
Recipe illustrations: Michael A Hill

CONTENTS

INTRODUCTION

Greetings! Dr. Hash here, the streetwise medicine man and Taoist master of weed. If, like me, you are partial to a regular snifter of marijuana and hashish, you'll be only too aware that smoking *anything* ain't good for you.

The good news is that you don't have to give up the joys of dope. You simply have to learn to cook with it! If you're a dab hand in the kitchen, and can easily whip together a three-course meal, you'll be laughing. If you can't, don't despair: the vast majority of recipes in this book are no more difficult than making a cup of coffee (you can do that, right?).

In no time you'll be the Nigella Lawson or Mario Batali of counterculture—the difference being, your dishes will give you and your dinner guests one hell of a buzz! And you can guarantee they'll be coming back for more.

My Infamous Aunt Mary Jane

I first tasted the joys of cooking with cannabis as a teenager in the 1960s. I grew up in London, but used to regularly visit my Aunt Mary Jane Belmore in San Francisco, where she lived from the early 1950s.

She was a high-society girl, but used to hang out with the beats. It was this experimental group of writers, along with local jazz musicians, who turned her on to weed. She was a non-smoker, but an avid cook, and soon took to cooking up cannabis dishes as a convenient and more pleasant way of taking the drug. Given her status in society, she was soon selling her cakes to the prim and proper housewives on Cisco's equivalent of Wisteria Lane.

Anyway, one time in 1965, when I was visiting Mary Jane (yes, that really was her name), she gave me one of her "cakes of light" for afternoon tea. It beat any sugar cookie I ever ate. Boy, did it light me up!

As I got older, I found myself becoming Mary Jane's apprentice on my trips to the West Coast of America. She initiated me into the art of cooking with cannabis. She showed me how to create Spaced-out Starters, Milky Way Main Courses, and Deep Space Desserts—not to mention Solar Snacks and Quantum Coffee.

I saw to it that I was a worthy pupil and literally lapped up the recipes she taught me. Put it this way, my head was on the far side of Venus on a daily basis.

The TV Chef and the Killer Weed

Back in the UK, I naturally practiced my new-found culinary art. At the same time, beginning at the age of 12, I learned the guitar. This made a killer combination. I was playing in bands and regularly going to gigs at the Roundhouse in Camden Town, London, watching bands like Led Zeppelin, The Doors, Incredible String Band, David Bowie, and later Motörhead. I ended up cooking dope recipes for many of the musicians in these bands, blowing their heads into deep space, through a black hole, and back to earth again. Perhaps unsurprisingly, I found myself in big demand.

I also got up to a great deal of mischief. In Britain there was a famous TV chef called Fanny Craddock. She was a household name and everyone had heard of her, whether they were interested in cooking or not.

One time, I put on a suit and talked my way into the TV studios where her shows were recorded live. When no one was looking, I sneaked into the kitchen section of the studio and dropped some of my famous cannabis-laced "Boom Boom Butter" into one of her creations.

Ten minutes later, dear old Fanny unwittingly cooked up a killer weed dish on live TV in full view of the nation! Towards the end of the show she and her husband Johnnie, who helped her on the show, tasted the dish.

Fanny said: "Mmmnn, lovely, don't you think, Johnnie?"

"Delicious," he replied.

As the show drew to a close, it was clear that Fanny and Johnnie were doing the fandango around Neptune and possibly talking to the machine elves of hyperspace to boot.

No one suspected anything, mainly because Fanny and Johnny were known as somewhat flamboyant characters, but I made a hasty exit from the studios, just in case...

"Howl"

Come the late 1970s, I was making my living playing in bands and selling rare and secondhand books. I used to spend part of the year in San Francisco, staying with Aunt Mary Jane, who by then was in her sixties, looking great, and still baking with mind-altering substances.

I recall going with her to an evening of poetry with beat writer Allen Ginsberg (1926–1997), who did a blistering rendition of his famous poem "Howl" at the City Lights bookstore in the North Beach/Chinatown area of Cisco.

After the reading, Mary Jane and I went up to talk with Allen. Mary knew him from the "beat days" of the 1950s, so Allen waved us through the throngs of people wanting to talk to him and get books signed.

"Well, well," he said in his New Jersey drawl. "If it isn't the infamous and highly improper Mary Jane!"

They hugged each other.

"How are you doing, Allen?" she said, handing him a Tupperware box of hash brownies. "Something to encourage your muses."

"Why, thank you," said Allen peering in the box and licking his lips at the sight of the hash cakes. "I'm flying out to Bill's bunker in New York tomorrow. I'll share them with him. He'll adore them." (He was referring to cult author William S. Burroughs, 1914–1997.)

Mary Jane was a big collector of books by the beat generation. She owned signed copies of William Burroughs' *Wild Boys* and *Cities of the Red Night*, Allen Ginsberg's *Howl*, and even an old exercise book full of scrawled notes inscribed by the king of the beats himself, Jack Kerouac (1922–1969).

As a book dealer, I was always trying to get Mary Jane to sell them to me— or at least leave them to me in her will. But she always used to say: "You little conniving pipsqueak! You'll be lucky to get one of my hop plants when I finally take my place in the underworld."

The Final Hours and My Aunt's Great Legacy

As it turned out, dear old Mary Jane passed in 2005. She'd moved out to Santa Cruz, partly on the recommendation of Robert Anton Wilson, the far-edge philosopher and author of the science fiction trilogy *Illuminatus!*, who had moved out there himself in his final years.

Mary Jane was 97 when she died and was eating hash cakes on her deathbed. She must have been high as the proverbial kite when she entered the next world. Her last words were: "I'm goin' on my biggest adventure yet ... I'll come back and see you if they hand out return-visit passes in hell."

I'd flown out to California a couple of days before she died. I was very grateful to have been able to spend the last few hours with the woman who had been my mentor for so long.

True to form, Mary Jane left me two things in her will: her cannabis cookbook, which consisted of three pencil-written exercise books, and a signed copy of William Burroughs' *The Cat Inside*. This was no surprise. Both Mary Jane and I had always loved cats, and Burroughs' book is perhaps the most profound and moving book ever written about felines.

As "witchdoctors of weed", we saw cats as our totem animals. And besides, Mary Jane and I were as rabid for weed as cats are for the herb catnip (the feline-world equivalent of marijuana).

I treasured Mary Jane's cannabis cookbook and often whipped up dishes from it for my friends and myself. What's more, my friends, and even friends of their friends, kept asking me for photocopies of the cookbook. It got to a point where I was spending my evenings at the copy shop!

In the end, I said: "I'm going to publish this as a book, complete with reminiscences of my Aunt Mary Jane and stories about my own adventures of cooking with weed."

This is the book you're holding in your hands... Enjoy it. And I'll meet you on the eastside of paradise!

Dr. Hash

September 23
HighTown Villas, London

THE BASICS:
KNOWING YOUR WEED

Word on the street

If you're going to cook with cannabis, or ingest it in any other form for that matter, you'll need to know your weed. *Cannabis sativa*, to give cannabis its Latin biological title, is known by many names, from marijuana (derived from the Spanish) to ganja (which comes from the Sanskrit word meaning "hemp").

On the street, of course, it's got dozens of slang names, from grass, pot, and reefer to dope, Mary Jane (M.J.), and weed.

A good many of us like to indulge in a little weed. According to the latest estimates, 4 per cent of the world's adults (162 million) use cannabis each year and 0.6 per cent (22.5 million) use it every day. That's a lot of people, especially when you consider that cannabis is an illegal drug in the majority of countries in the world.

So why do people take it if they run the risk of a visit from the cops? What's so special about the cannabis plant?

My old friend, Canadian shaman and expert on mind-altering plants, Elias Crazywolf (www.wolfshaman.com), makes no bones about it: "It's down to the fact that us humans like—or even actually need—to get high on a regular basis. We need to get off our faces to appreciate the world around us, otherwise we take it for granted."

What drugs do, explains Elias, is allow us to experience a separate reality that coexists with our own. "It's the world shamans see when they enter ritualistic trance and commune with the spirits," he says.

The history of getting high

If you look back at the history of cannabis, you discover there's evidence for its use as a mind-altering substance as far back as the third millennium BCE. An artifact known as a "pipe cup" was found in a pit-grave burial in Romania, along with a similar pipe cup at a north Caucasian early Bronze Age site. Both pipes contained the charred remnants of cannabis seeds. A great number of hemp seeds have also been found at Neolithic sites in central Europe.

Cannabis was used widely in the ancient Near East. It was used by the Assyrians to relieve sorrow and grief, which shows they viewed it as a way of lifting the spirits—or in other words a way of getting "high." The Assyrians called it *qunubu* ("way to produce smoke"), which some believe may have been the origin of the modern word cannabis.

Shamans, known as "kapnobatai," from the Thracian/Dacian (Greece and the Balkans) cultures in the third and second millennia BCE used cannabis flowers to induce a state of trance. It is thought that this practice was inherited by Greek oracles and worshippers, including members of the Dionysus mystery cult.

In 2003, a leather basket filled with cannabis leaf fragments and seeds was found next to a 2,700-year-old mummified shaman at the Yanghai Tombs near Turpan, Xinjiang-Uighur Autonomous Region, in China.

Cannabis has also been used by Muslims in various Sufi and Whirling Dervish orders. Some authorities claim it was used as a religious sacrament by the ancient Jews and early Christians.

The active ingredient

The reason cannabis has been used such a lot in magical and religious rites—or simply to get high and have a good time—is down to its active ingredient tetrahydrocannabinol, thankfully otherwise known as THC.

THC is basically a psychoactive chemical that alters perception and produces feelings of euphoria and relaxation. On the negative side, it can induce feelings of paranoia and anxiety. I've only ever seen this happen in people that have existing psychological issues—and once in an otherwise balanced guy who was going through a severe bout of depression.

Know your cannabis

Cannabis comes in different forms, most of which can be used in cooking. The three main types are listed below.

MARIJUANA: This is the dried flowers, leaves, and seeds from the female cannabis plant. It's the least potent form of cannabis and is usually smoked, but you can also sprinkle it in food or make a tea from it.

HYDROPONIC WEED: This is marijuana grown indoors under controlled conditions to produce plants that are considerably stronger than traditional grass. Hydroponic weed has become increasingy common and can be used in the same way as normal marijuana but it is potent stuff so reduce the amount you put in your recipes.

HASHISH: This is made from the resin (secreted gum) of the female cannabis plant. The resin is dried and pressed into small blocks. Again, this can be smoked or added to food. If you are partial to hashish, you shouldn't store it for too long or it will lose a lot of its potency.

HASH OIL: This is the most potent form of cannabis—a thick oil, usually sold in small vials. Dissolving the hashish in solvents, like acetone, alcohol, butane, or petroleum ether, creates this oil. The resulting liquid is then separated from any plant matter and the solvent is allowed to evaporate, leaving the sticky oil.

Quantities

The big problem with dope in all its varieties is that it is not regulated. This means you can't be sure of the potency from one batch to the next. When you use this book, it will be up to you how much you decide to use. As a general guide, use 2 grams of good-quality cannabis per person, and if in doubt always err on the side of caution. Remember, if you're not as stoned as you want to be you can always eat or smoke some more, but it doesn't work the other way round. Where the recipes suggest using marijuana, please note this is traditional weed not a hydroponic variety. If you are using hydroponics stick to around 2–3 grams per person. It's also important that you take dope with people you trust.

The healing herb

Cannabis isn't just about getting high. It's also a medicinal herb. Unfortunately, the laws in most countries do not take the therapeutic qualities into account. This hasn't stopped 70-year-old grandmother Patricia Tabram from cooking up cannabis dishes to ease her health problems. She has used cannabis to relieve the depression she has suffered since the death of her son Duncan in 1975. She says eating the drug also helps combat the aches and pains she suffers as a result of two car crashes.

Patricia says the drug had an almost immediate impact: "I had a walking stick, I was in constant pain. Now, through ingesting cannabis in my food five times a day, five times a week—minute amounts—I feel great."

Her book *Grandma Eats Cannabis* details how she keeps jars of cannabis powder in her kitchen, dope-laced food in her freezer, and how she regularly whips up cannabis-laced curries, casseroles, and ice cream. I have to say, Aunt Mary Jane would have loved Patricia. And I'm sure they would have shared a few recipes!

Boom Boom Butter

Before you begin cooking with cannabis you need to learn how to turn it into butter. Although you can just throw some marijuana leaves into a dish—like you would with mixed herbs—you'll get better results, both in terms of taste and potency, by cooking with a bit of Boom Boom Butter. This is because the main psychoactive chemical in cannabis (THC) needs to first be extracted into fat (butter or oil) or alcohol to produce the optimum effect.

Once you've made your butter, you can use it in almost any recipe, from spaghetti Bolognese, chili, and curry to cakes, biscuits, and cookies. So, let's make some of my Aunt Mary Jane's Boom Boom Butter!

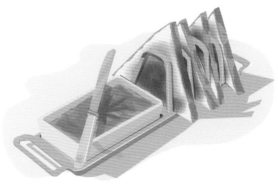

You will need:

1 stick (8 tablespoons) butter

¼ oz (8–10 g) cannabis, chopped or ground (as ever, the amount depends on the quality of the cannabis you have)

measuring jug

pint glass

1. Pour 2½ cups (595 ml) water into a saucepan and bring to a boil.

2. Add the butter and stir until melted.

3. Add the cannabis to the water and butter mixture and stir.

4. Simmer for 30 minutes, making sure the pan doesn't boil dry. Only a small amount of water should have evaporated from the pan.

5. Strain the liquid into a pint glass.

6. Put the glass in the fridge until two layers form. The top (solid) layer is your Boom Boom Butter, ready to use in any way you wish. Discard the bottom layer.

7. You could start by spreading some on a slice of toast in the morning. Boom! You'll be stratospheric before lunchtime!

In case you were wondering, Aunt Mary Jane called her cannabis butter "Boom Boom" after the 1961 song "Boom Boom" by famed Mississippi bluesman, John Lee Hooker (1917–2001). In fact, we both loved John's music. I spent many a long hour learning John's deep haunting riffs on my guitar, while Mary Jane cooked up her potent dishes.

COOL BEGINNINGS

Out-of-this-world Avocado Dip

Although Aunt Mary Jane lived in the chilled-out world of San Francisco, she kept elements of her English roots, which meant she was always very particular. She liked to do things with proper decorum. Dinner was served at 8.00 p.m. sharp. There was also no such thing as "tea"—the term used by the English working classes to describe their evening meal or dinner. It had to be *dinner*, and never tea.

Mary Jane did, however, serve afternoon tea, which was a different thing altogether.

Served around 4.00 p.m., it typically consisted of a pot of tea (loose tea, not tea bags) and scones—pronounced with a long "o" (as in "oh"), never with a short one.

As you might expect, dinner had to begin with an appetizer. Mary Jane would have been horrified at the thought of diving right into the entrée without, at the very least, a soup first.

One of my favorite appetizers of Mary Jane's was her Avocado Dip. It's easy to make, and it's a great introduction to cooking with cannabis.

You will need:

3 tablespoons white wine

½ cup (30 g) marijuana, finely chopped

2 teaspoons chili powder

3 ripe avocados

1 large onion, finely chopped

1. Mix the wine, marijuana, and chili powder together in a bowl. Let the mixture stand for an hour.

2. Add the avocados and onion. Mash it all together with a wooden spoon.

3. This is perfect served with tortilla chips.

Galactic Garlic Bread

You will need:

1 French stick

2 garlic cloves, crushed

2 teaspoons Boom Boom Butter

¼ stick (2 tablespoons) regular butter

1. This is an easy recipe to master. Cut a French stick in half. Put the crushed garlic and Boom Boom Butter in a bowl. Add a ¼ stick (2 tablespoons) of regular butter.

2. Mix it all together and spread it on the cut side of the French stick. Wrap the bread in aluminum foil and put it in the oven for ten minutes at 350°F (180°C/gas 4).

3. Serve immediately, and get ready to fly!

Far-out Falafels

When it comes to etiquette, I'm far more casual in my approach than Mary Jane ever was. Nevertheless, I've always felt that it's good manners to maintain certain standards— even when you are ingesting illegal substances. In the words of Mary Jane: "After all, we are not a crack house."

One time in the 1990s, when I was staying with Mary Jane, Billy Cobb, a cop with the Los Angeles Police Department (LAPD), and friends—paid us a visit. I always remember him telling us: *"I truly love my job. Nothing beats blasting down a crack house door with a pump-action shotgun—the rush is indescribable."*

Although she took drugs herself, pretty much on a daily basis, she considered it a dignified, almost spiritual way of life—a far cry from the life of a crack head. Mary Jane was essentially a shamaness of San Francisco society culture.

Naturally, she didn't share this aspect of her life with Billy. But being rather mischievous, she did invite him to dinner one evening. The meal began with her famous starter—red lentil and chickpea falafel, laced with marijuana.

Being health conscious and a body builder, Billy thoroughly enjoyed the falafels. *"Mary Jane,"* he said, *"you gotta gimme the recipe."*

Half-an-hour later, Billy was space-truckin' around the Milky Way and had lost all interest in pump-action shotguns, pumping iron, and raiding crack houses. From that day on, he always eyed Mary Jane with suspicion—and he never ever accepted a dinner invitation from her again.

You will need:

3 cups (675 g) chickpeas, soaked overnight

2 cups (450 g) red lentils

2½ cups (595 ml) vegetable stock

1 medium onion, finely chopped

2 garlic cloves, crushed

1 teaspoon ground cumin

1 teaspoon ground coriander

olive oil for frying

1 cup (100 g) rolled oats, plus extra for coating

1 cup (60 g) marijuana, finely chopped

salt and freshly ground black pepper

1. Boil the chickpeas in water until soft. Leave to stand. Add the lentils to the vegetable stock. Simmer gently for approximately 15 minutes until all the stock is absorbed and the lentils are tender. Put to one side.

2. Fry the onion, garlic, cumin, and coriander in olive oil, until the onion and garlic are soft and slightly browned.

3. Purée the chickpeas in a blender. Mix together the chickpeas, red lentils, onion, garlic, cumin, coriander, oats, and marijuana in a bowl, and add salt and black pepper to taste. Set aside a small bowl of oats for shallow frying later.

4. Leave to stand in a cool place for 30 minutes, or until the mixture becomes firm. Then work the mixture into small patties. Dip each one in the oats and shallow fry in olive oil until they are golden brown.

5. Serve with salad and mayonnaise.

Killa Dawg's Cosmic Crackers

Most of us are just too damned busy to cook these days, so quick and easy ways to prepare blow—and regular food, for that matter—are essential.

I was talking about this just the other week, in fact. I was in The Silver Star, a bar in West London, with a good friend of mine—the rapper Killa Dawg. Because it's not good for your health, he gave up smoking weed in favor of cooking it about a year ago.

His specialty is quick cannabis snacks. If dope wasn't illegal, he'd have opened a fast-food joint for marijuana.

Way I see it," he said over a vodka on the rocks, *"is you want a quick hit, like you get with a drive-thru burger joint. You want it fast. You don't want to mess about with gourmet s***."*

Aunt Mary Jane would not have approved. She believed dope should be savored in food, not treated like a TV dinner.

Nevertheless, the Killa had a good point.

With Young Jeezy's classic "Circulate" playing on the jukebox, he took off his aviator-style sunglasses and told me how to make his favorite weed snack, which can easily double as a canapé for serving to dinner guests or for an informal soirée.

You will need:

wheat crackers

chocolate spread

1 cup (60 g) marijuana leaves, finely chopped

1. Spread a generous helping of chocolate spread onto two crackers.

2. Sprinkle some marijuana on top of this.

3. Put the crackers together to make a sandwich.

4. Place on a baking sheet and cook for 20 minutes at 325°F (170°C/gas 3).

5. Serve straight away.

Alternatively, spread some Boom Boom Butter on the crackers before adding the chocolate spread and then cook them as above.

Bread of Poetry

Another great starter, which is a bit more complicated than Cosmic Crackers, is dope-laced cinnamon bread, or Mary Jane's Bread of Poetry. It was a favorite of hers throughout the 1970s. She'd often prepare it for the small literary functions she held at her San Francisco house on Wednesday afternoons. It certainly got the juices of the artistic crowd flowing!

"Only thing was," she told me with a sigh, "they weren't all exactly gifted poets, so when the moment came to read their work out loud, it was a good thing we were all stoned."

You will need:

2 cups (230 g) all-purpose (plain) flour

1 cup (225 g) brown sugar

2 teaspoons baking powder

½ teaspoon bicarbonate of soda

1½ teaspoons ground cinnamon

½ teaspoon salt

1 cup (240 ml) buttermilk

¼ cup (60 ml) vegetable oil

2 eggs

2 teaspoons vanilla extract

2 teaspoons regular butter

4 teaspoons Boom Boom Butter

TOPPING

2 tablespoons sugar

1 teaspoon cinnamon

1 teaspoon regular butter

9 x 5 x 3-inch (23 x 13 x 7-cm) loaf tin

1. Preheat the oven to 350°F (180°C/gas 4).

2. Grease the loaf tin.

3. Place the flour, sugar, baking powder, bicarbonate of soda, cinnamon, salt, buttermilk, vegetable oil, eggs, vanilla extract, butter, and Boom Boom Butter in a mixing bowl.

4. Beat the mixture vigorously for about 3 minutes.

5. Pour the mixture into the loaf tin. Smooth the top of the mixture with a table knife.

6. Now turn your attention to the topping. Mix the sugar, cinnamon, and butter together until it forms a crumbly texture. Sprinkle this over the top of the loaf. Use a knife to create a swirly pattern on top of the loaf before placing it in the oven.

7. Bake the loaf for 50 minutes.

8. Test whether the loaf is properly cooked by pushing a knife into the center. It should come out clean if the loaf is ready to be removed from the oven.

Take Me Higher Tzatziki

This Greek-style appetizer was another favorite of Mary Jane's, which she loved to serve to guests in the early evening. It's not quite the authentic Greek recipe, what with the Boom Boom Butter, but it goes down well. You can always throw in some finely chopped marijuana if the Boom Boom Butter doesn't work for you.

You will need:

2 cartons plain yogurt

2 cucumbers, peeled and seeded

2 tablespoons Boom Boom Butter

$^1/_2$ lemon, freshly squeezed

1 tablespoon fresh dill, chopped

3 garlic cloves, crushed

salt and freshly ground black pepper

1. Blend the yogurt, cucumber, Boom Boom Butter, lemon juice, dill, garlic, and salt and pepper in a food processor until the mixture is relatively smooth.

2. Transfer it to a dish, cover, and refrigerate for at least an hour before serving.

3. This dip is great for dipping carrot sticks, cauliflower florets, and breadsticks. It will certainly get your guests in the mood for a party.

Stoned Salmon

A nice addition to any dope cook's cuisine is salmon with dope and dill sauce. It's light and tasty. If you're a purist, you can cure the salmon yourself, but that can be quite a long process. The quickest and easiest way is to use smoked salmon.

You will need:

2 tablespoons Dijon mustard

1 tablespoon superfine (caster) sugar

1 egg yolk

1 cup (240 ml) vegetable or groundnut oil, plus extra for drizzling

4 tablespoons fresh dill, chopped

a sprinkle of marijuana, finely chopped (add more for a stronger effect)

1 tablespoon white wine vinegar

1 packet smoked salmon

salt and freshly ground black pepper

1. In a large bowl, whisk the mustard and sugar together with the egg yolk. Slowly whisk in a steady trickle of oil, making sure the oil is well emulsified. Add the fresh dill, marijuana, and vinegar, and mix well.

2. Place 3–4 slices of smoked salmon on a plate along with a spoonful of the sauce. Serve with rye bread.

SWEET 'N' SMALL TREATS

Sweet Candy Hash Balls

When it comes to sweet, small, and succulent treats, the all-time master is Filthy Phil Edmonds. His culinary skills don't beat Aunt Mary Jane's, of course, but there's no doubt that he comes a close second.

In fact, you might know Phil. He's a veteran of the festival circuit, both in the US and the UK. He's been to just about every festival going, and is one of those people who seems to know everyone.

Why is he nicknamed "filthy"? Well, it's down to the Volkswagen Camper Van he drives. He's never washed it since he bought it in 1969! He claims it still has mud on it from the very first Glastonbury Festival in 1970 (it was actually called the Pilton Festival that year and 1,500 people attended). The headline act was Tyrannosaurus Rex, who later transformed into legendary glam rockers T. Rex, led by Marc Bolan.

Try not to get the wrong impression about Filthy Phil. In every other way, he is meticulous about cleanliness. Even though it's far from easy in a confined space, Phil showers and shampoos his long hair (now grey) on a daily basis in his VW.

During the 1980s, I went to Glasto a number of times with Phil. In the evenings, just as the sun was setting over the Somerset Levels, he would rustle up some Sweet Candy Hash Balls. These are utterly delicious, and you certainly won't be suffering from munchies after eating your way through a batch of these!

Phil's Sweet Candy Hash Balls used to attract quite a crowd, who would gather around our campfire munching them and getting seriously stoned. Wow! They were some evenings!

In the distance you could hear the headline acts, which included Dr. John, The Smiths, and Weather Report.

If I remember correctly, that was 1984. But for me the previous year, 1983, was the killer year—with Curtis Mayfield (1949–1999) headlining.

You should have heard his rendition of his classic "Superfly." That was part of the soundtrack of the superb 1972 movie Superfly with Ron O'Neal as Youngblood Priest, a black coke dealer trying to quit New York's drug underworld.

Curtis Mayfield had a very unusual style. Not only did he sing falsetto, he tuned his guitar to an open F# A# C# F# A# F#—the same notes as the black keys on the piano. That was innovative, and was a big contributor to his unique sound.

You will need:

2 cups (450 g) roasted cashew nut butter

a handful of currants

3–4 tablespoons of honey

2 cups (230 g) shredded coconut

½ cup (55 g) ground almonds

1 cup (60 g) pulverized cannabis (use a pestle and mortar to do this), or flake in some Lebanese hash

1. Put all the ingredients into a mixing bowl and knead together.

2. Roll out the mixture onto a board and make as many marble-sized balls as possible from the mixture.

3. Put the sweet candy balls on a plate and leave in the refrigerator overnight. Remove from the fridge just before serving.

Yogurt Pot

You will need:

a pinch of hash, crumbled (depending on how stoned you want to get)

oil for frying

1 pot plain yogurt

honey, to drizzle

a handful of chopped strawberries or blueberries

1. Crumble the hash into a spoonful of oil in a skillet (frying pan), then gently heat the oil until the hash melts. Take the pot of yogurt and stir in a teaspoonful of the hash oil, then pour into a serving bowl and add honey and fruit to taste.

2. If you're in a hurry, you can just buy a pot of fruit yogurt and stir in the hash oil, and eat straight from the pot.

Classic Hash Brownies

Going back to Filthy Phil, he had one of the very best recipes for the cannabis cuisine classic—hash brownies. He'd rustle some of these up in his VW in no time.

People were always saying to him,
"Hey Filthy, when you going make some more of your hash brownies?"

"When I'm good and ready," he'd say.
"But I promise you, I'll put some together before I clean my van."

You will need:

Makes 16 pieces

½ cup (55 g) self-rising flour

½ teaspoon baking powder

⅓ cup (42 g) cocoa powder

¼ cup (25 g) ground almonds

1 cup (225 g) soft brown sugar

rind of 1 large orange, grated

8 tablespoons Boom Boom Butter

2 eggs

CHOCOLATE FROSTING

1 stick (8 tablespoons) regular butter or margarine

½–1 cup (25–55 g) cocoa powder

2–2¼ cups (225–275 g) confectioner's (icing) sugar

shallow dish

waxed paper

1. Sift the flour, baking powder, and cocoa powder into a large mixing bowl.

2. Add the ground almonds, sugar, and orange rind, and thoroughly mix together.

3. Add the butter and eggs, and then beat the mixture together until smooth.

4. Bake at 300°F (150°C/gas 2) in a shallow dish, greased with butter and lined with waxed paper, for about 50 minutes.

5. Leave to cool while you make the chocolate frosting.

6. For the frosting, mix together the ingredients in a bowl and then spread it on top of the brownies.

7. Lastly, cut the brownies into 16 pieces and serve.

Gilbert the Roadie's Peanut Butter Cookies

In one of the bands I played in during the 1980s, The Dying Breed, we had a roadie called Gilbert. That really was his name! Anyway, Gilbert was a pit bull for dope. He could smell it a mile away, and once he got his teeth into it there was no shaking him. He truly loved his weed. Gilbert liked to smoke it either as a joint or from a bong.

He also cooked with cannabis. He used to make some outstanding hash cookies. I scribbled down his recipe one evening, after we'd finished a gig in Bristol's Western Star Domino Club. Opposite is the certified original.

You will need:

Makes about 12 cookies

½ cup (110 g) peanut butter

12 tablespoons Boom Boom Butter

1¼ cups (175 g) all-purpose (plain) flour

1 egg, beaten

½ teaspoon vanilla extract

½ teaspoon baking soda

½ cup (110 g) brown sugar

¼ teaspoon salt

a handful of grated milk chocolate

a handful of shredded coconut

1. Mix together all the ingredients, except the coconut, in a bowl. Knead the mixture until it forms a dough texture.

2. Create as many cookies as you can from the mixture. Put them on a baking sheet.

3. Bake in the oven at 350°F (180°C/gas 4) for about 30 minutes, or until the edges of the cookies are slightly browned.

4. Take the cookies out of the oven and sprinkle with the shredded coconut.

5. Leave to cool, or serve directly.

Paradise Pancakes

Likeable though Gilbert was, he had a serious failing—he was lazy. He had the uncanny knack of disappering when the band needed him to move amps and speakers. This was unfortunate, seeing as shifting gear made up the bulk of his job description.

One time, everyone in the band got together and decided we'd show Gilbert the error of his ways.

I said to Gilbert, "Hey, Gil, can you shift the amps and cabs over to the practice studios? If you can get it done by lunchtime, there's a big lump of Red Leb in it for you."

I could see the pit-bull hunger in his eyes. "Oh wow, man, I'm on to it." *With that he shot out of the door. Red Leb was a 100 percent guaranteed cure for his lazyitis.*

What Gilbert didn't know was I'd earlier put some dumbbells in the back of the speaker cabs, making them impossible to lift, unless, of course, you had a forklift truck handy. About an hour later, Gilbert returned red faced and sweating like a dog.

"Hey, man," *he said.* "Something strange is going down. I couldn't move those cabs. Either they've put on weight or I'm on some kinda weird s*** acid trip."

He then grimaced in pain, adding, "And I think I've done my back in."

The truth was, Gilbert had got his just desserts. But I couldn't help feeling guilty about the trick I'd played on him, so that night I cooked him up one of the most delicious recipes my Aunt Mary Jane ever taught me. This is it. Try it yourself, and you'll love it.

𝒴𝒐𝒖 𝒘𝒊𝒍𝒍 𝒏𝒆𝒆𝒅:

Makes about 10 pancakes

1½ cups (250 g) all-purpose (plain) flour

2 teaspoons baking powder

3 tablespoons sugar

1 teaspoon salt

small pinch cinnamon

2 eggs, lightly beaten

1 cup (250 ml) milk

½ stick (4 tablespoons) Boom Boom Butter, melted, plus extra for cooking (when I cooked it up for Gilbert, I used the Red Lebanese hash)

1. Place the flour, baking powder, sugar, and salt in a large bowl. Mix the eggs, milk, and metled Boom Boom Butter in a large pitcher, then add to the other ingredients and mix to make the batter. Preheat a skillet (frying pan) or griddle while making the batter.

2. Add a chunk of butter to the skillet or griddle. Pour in about 3 tablespoons of the mixture to create your first pancake. Fry one side, and then flip over and fry the other side. Serve with lemon juice and sugar to taste.

Gysin's Classic Hash Fudge

You remember I told you that Aunt Mary Jane knew the cult author, William S. Burroughs? Well, one of Bill Burroughs' friends during the years he lived in Morocco was Brion Gysin (1916–1986), a British-born surrealist painter and poet.

As a joke, Gysin contributed a recipe for marijuana fudge to a cookbook by San Francisco-born writer and socialite, Alice B. Toklas. It was first published in 1954 and has been in print ever since. The recipe was unintentionally included for publication, becoming famous under the name Alice B. Toklas' brownies. This is the recipe. Try it and see what you think.

You will need:

1 cup (225 g) sugar

1 whole nutmeg, crushed

4 sticks cinnamon, crushed

1 teaspoon coriander, crushed

¼ teaspoon black peppercorns, crushed

a handful of stoned dates, chopped

a handful of dried figs, chopped

a handful of ground almonds

4 tablespoons Boom Boom Butter

1. Heat up a pat of regular butter in a saucepan and when melted, mix in the sugar until it dissolves.

2. Mix all of the remaining ingredients together in a bowl, along with a good helping of Boom Boom Butter. Add the dissolved sugar mix and stir.

3. Roll the mixture into an oblong and cut into small blocks.

4. Refrigerate for a few hours, then serve. Two blocks will probably be all you'll need!

Gysin described his recipe as "the food of Paradise," adding that:

"...it might provide an entertaining refreshment for a Ladies' Bridge Club or a chapter meeting of the DAR [Daughters of the American Revolution]... Euphoria and brilliant storms of laughter; ecstatic reveries and extensions of one's personality on several simultaneous planes are to be complacently expected. Almost anything Saint Theresa did, you can do better."

Sky-high Shortbread

Aunt Mary Jane originally came from Britain, so it's no surprise that she loved to make shortbread and serve it up with afternoon tea. If you fancy a little pick-me-up with your tea, then give this a try. It's delicious.

You will need:

½ stick (4 tablespoons) regular butter

4 tablespoons Boom Boom Butter

1¼ cups (175 g) all-purpose (plain) flour

¼ cup (50 g) superfine (caster) sugar

Makes about 24 rounds or 32 fingers

1. Beat the butter, Boom Boom Butter, and sugar into a pale-looking mixture.

2. Stir in the flour to make a smooth paste dough (or mixture). Place the dough on a board or work surface. Roll it out until it's about ½ inch (2 cm) thick.

3. Cut the dough into rounds or fingers. Sprinkle with a little sugar.

4. Place on a baking sheet and chill in the refrigerator for 20 minutes.

5. Bake in the oven at 375°F (180°C/gas 5) for 15–20 minutes, until the shortbread is a pale golden color.

6. Leave to cool on a wire rack. Serve with afternoon tea.

Fabulous Flip-out Flapjacks

Flapjacks are a great sweet treat at any time of day. They'll satisfy your hunger pangs, as well as give you a little bit more than a sugar buzz...

You will need:

Makes about 12 pieces

3 oz (6 tablespoons) regular butter

4 tablespoons Boom Boom Butter

¼ cup (50 g) superfine (caster) sugar

¼ cup (60 ml) clear honey, plus a little extra for drizzling

2 cups (200 g) oats

waxed paper

confectioner's (icing) sugar to dust

1. Put the butter, Boom Boom Butter, sugar, honey, and oats in a bowl. Mix thoroughly.

2. Line a baking sheet with the waxed paper and spoon the flapjack mixture onto the sheet.

3. Place them in the oven and cook for 10 minutes at 400°F (200°C/gas 6).

4. Remove the flapjacks from the oven and transfer them into a freezer for 5 minutes to set and firm.

5. Once the flapjacks have set, remove them from the freezer and cut into equal-sized chunks.

6. To serve, put the flapjacks on a plate, dust with confectioners' sugar, and drizzle with honey.

BIG STUFF

Steak with Weed

Late one evening, I was telling my friend Ray about how I'd learned the art of cooking with cannabis from my Aunt Mary Jane.

"No s**t," he said. *"She like hip-hop?"* he asked.

"She did," I replied. *"Her roots were in jazz, which was a very radical and innovative musical form, very much like the best in hip-hop, which breaks new ground."*

I told him how Mary knew some of the South Central LA hip-hop crews, through one of her artist friends.

"She used to say that Ice Cube wouldn't be who he is today, if she hadn't given him her grilled steak with weed recipe."

You will need:

Serves 4

4 good-quality steaks

1 teaspoon olive oil

Boom Boom Butter for seasoning

2 garlic cloves, crushed

2 teaspoons fresh rosemary, chopped

2 teaspoons fresh thyme, chopped

2 teaspoons fresh basil, chopped

freshly ground black pepper

1. Place the steaks in a shallow dish. Rub both sides with the oil, Boom Boom Butter, garlic, and herbs and season with black pepper. Let stand for one hour.

2. Prepare the skillet (frying pan) with a little olive oil. Cook the steaks to the desired "doneness," usually 4 minutes per side if you like them rare. Personally, I like steak fairly well done, so I cook it for about 20 minutes.

"You're putting me on," said Ray.

"Well, I might be," I replied with a wink, then gave him the recipe anyway to add to his own cannabis cuisine repertoire.

Satan's Own Spaghetti Bolognese

Aunt Mary Jane wasn't the only unusual character to inhabit the streets of San Francisco. One of her friends was Anton Lavey, founder of the Church of Satan. "Anton was far from devilish," she told me in 1997 after Lavey died. "He was one of the most decent and honorable people you would ever care to meet. And he absolutely adored animals (he famously had a pet lion)."

Anton wasn't big on drugs, but, as Aunt Mary Jane put it, "He made a mean spaghetti Bolognese." It's no surprise that Mary Jane promptly adapted Anton's recipe for cannabis. It's great!

You will need:

Serves 6–8

2 tablespoons olive oil

6 slices smoked streaky bacon, finely chopped

3 lb (1.25 kg) ground beef

2 large onions, roughly chopped

3 garlic cloves, crushed

2 large glasses red wine

2 large cans chopped tomatoes

¼ lb (125 g) button mushrooms, quartered

2 bay leaves

1 teaspoon chopped fresh oregano

1 teaspoon chopped fresh thyme

½ cup (30 g) marijuana, finely chopped (or 2–3 tablespoons Boom Boom Butter)

balsamic vinegar to drizzle

12–14 sundried tomato halves in oil, chopped

1 teaspoon chopped fresh basil

1 packet spaghetti

Parmesan cheese to serve

salt and freshly ground black pepper

1. Heat the olive oil in a large pan over medium heat.

2. Fry the bacon and ground beef until browned.

3. Add the onion and garlic, and fry until soft.

4. Pour in the red wine. Boil until the liquid has reduced in volume by about a third.

5. Reduce the temperature. Stir in the tomatoes, mushrooms, bay leaves, oregano, thyme, marijuana, and balsamic vinegar.

6. Add sundried tomatoes and season with black pepper and salt.

7. Cover the pan with lid. Simmer for 1–1½ hours, stirring occasionally, until the sauce is rich and thick.

8. At the end of the cooking, stir in the basil.

9. Remove from the heat and allow the sauce to "settle." In the meantime, cook the spaghetti in plenty of boiling salted water. Read packet for instructions on cooking time.

10. Drain the spaghetti, and serve on warmed plates.

11. Ladle on the Bolognese sauce.

12. Scatter the Parmesan over the spaghetti Bolognese and add a twist of black pepper.

Boom Boom Veggie Breakfast

Aunt Mary Jane often mixed with
the artistic crowd in San Franciso,
many of whom were vegetarians.
She was always ready to rustle up a
non-meat dish, if the need arose.
One of my favorites was this mix
of eggs, onion, and mushrooms.

You will need:

Serves 6–8

1 teaspoon vegetable oil

1 medium onion, finely sliced

10–12 medium white button mushrooms, quartered

4 tablespoons Boom Boom Butter

12 hard-boiled eggs, peeled and chopped

freshly ground black pepper

1. Fry the onions in the oil until they are golden brown.

2. Add the mushrooms and Boom Boom Butter and fry for another 5 minutes, stirring frequently, until the mushrooms become soft.

3. Remove from heat and let cool.

4. Mix together with the eggs and season with the black pepper.

5. Chill until ready to serve.

Chicken Surprise

You don't need to be an amazing chef to pull this recipe off. It's just roast chicken and vegetables all thrown in the oven. You can leave it to cook while you have a good time with your dinner guests.

You will need:

Serves 4

1 medium-sized whole chicken (4½ lb/2 kg)

4 bacon slices

1 stick (8 tablespoons) regular butter, cut into small chunks

1 tablespoon oregano, chopped

1 cup (60 g) marijuana, finely chopped

freshly ground black pepper

10 small potatoes, scrubbed

8 small carrots, scrubbed

4 parsnips, scrubbed and quartered

1 large onion, peeled and quartered

1. Preheat the oven to 400°F (200°C/gas 6).

2. Wash the cavity of the chicken under cold water, and pat dry with kitchen paper. Place the chicken in a roasting dish. Layer bacon slices over the top, and add some chunks of butter. Twist a good measure of black pepper over the top, and sprinkle over the oregano and marijuana. While you're doing this, you may as well crumble on some hash, too! Let's go all out!

3. Next, add the potatoes, carrots, parsnips, and onion (or other vegetables of your choice) to the roasting dish alongside the chicken.

4. A medium-sized chicken usually takes a couple of hours to cook. To be certain it's cooked, stick a knife in the thickest part of the thigh and make sure the juices are running clear. Then remove the chicken from the oven. Put it on a plate to rest for 10 minutes.

5. Serve with the roasted vegetables for a real roast high.

Haricot Bean Hash

You will need:

Serves 4

butter for frying

olive oil for frying

1 onion, finely chopped

1 garlic clove, crushed

small pinch chili powder

1 tablespoon tomato paste

just under ⅛ cup
(8 g hash), crumbled

1 can haricot beans

freshly ground black pepper

1. There's nothing like homemade baked beans, something us Brits are all too familiar with. It beats what you get out of a tin, any day. Melt the butter and olive oil in a skillet (frying pan), on low heat. Add the onion and crushed garlic. Fry in the pan until soft.

2. Now add the chili powder, a few twists of black pepper, the tomato paste, and, most importantly, crumble in some hash. Mix everything together into a paste, and add around 2 tablespoons of water to stop the paste from being too thick.

3. Now drain a can of haricot beans and add them to the pan. Cook gently for 5 or 10 minutes.

4. Serve with toast.

Ace of Spades Chili con Carne

You remember I was telling you about Gilbert the roadie, earlier? Well, his long-term girlfriend was a very nice, down-to-earth lady called Layla. She kept Gilbert on the straight and narrow, and stopped him going off the rails.

There was one time when I remember saying to her that I'd bumped into Lemmy of Motörhead at a gig a few weeks before.

"Oh, wow," she said. *"How's he doing?"*

"He's doing great," I replied. *"Do you know him?"*

"You could say that," she said. *"I slept with all of Hawkwind."* (Lemmy was a member of Hawkwind before forming Motörhead).

That was a conversation stopper … but I thought quickly, and said: "All at the same time? Or individually?"

"Separately," she replied, laughing. *What do you take me for?!"*

Rather appropriately, Layla had a great dope recipe she called Ace of Spades Chili con Carne, named after the classic Motörhead song from 1980. It's got enough spice and weed to put you in orbit around Mars. Treat with great caution...

You will need:

Serves 2–3

1 lb (450 g) ground beef

Extra-virgin olive oil for frying

2 onions, roughly chopped

2 garlic cloves, crushed

2 teaspoons chili powder

a handful of marijuana, finely chopped

2 tablespoons tomato paste

1 can tomatoes

1 can red kidney beans

a handful of dark chocolate, grated

plain yogurt and rice to serve

1. Fry the ground beef in olive oil. When it's browned, add the onions and garlic.

2. Add the chili powder and marijuana. Then fry for another minute before adding the tomato paste, canned tomatoes, red kidney beans, and dark chocolate.

3. Cook for about 45 minutes.

4. Serve on a bed of rice, topped with a spoonful of plain yogurt.

Loco Chili Cheese and Hash Nachos

I'm a big fan of Tex Mex cuisine. Nachos are one of my favorites, mainly because they make a great fast meal. If you add a little bit of hash, it gives them that extra touch of heaven.

The dish was invented in 1943 by the maître d' at the Victory Club restaurant in Piedras Negras, Coahuila, Mexico, close to the Texas border. Some people came in late, just as the place was about to close. The maître d' saw to it they had something to eat by using up any ingredients he had left, so he made up a dish with fried tortilla chips covered with cheese and jalapeño peppers. It went down a treat with his late-night guests. The recipe soon spread over to Texas and as far as Los Angeles. In 1954, the original recipe was included in the St. Anne's Cookbook.

Hey, with all this talk, I'm getting hungry. Let's make some dope-laced nachos!

You will need:

Serves 6

7 oz (200 g) tortilla chips

2 large tomatoes, roughly chopped

1 cup (250 g) grated mozzarella

2 large green chilies, seeded
and sliced

just over ⅛ cup (12 g) hash, crumbled

freshly ground black pepper

1. Preheat the oven to 400°F
(200°C/gas 6).

2. Place the tortilla chips on a
nonstick baking sheet.

3. Top with the chopped tomatoes
and the mozzarella.

4. Scatter over the green chilies
and hash.

5. Season generously with freshly
ground black pepper.

6. Put the tortillas in the oven
for 5–8 minutes until the cheese
is bubbling and the top is
beginning to brown.

7. Transfer the tortillas to a
large plate.

8. If you're feeling brave, serve
with the Out-of-this-world Avocado
Dip on page 16.

Happy Hash Pizza

Mary Jane also made a mean hash pizza. Not only is it tasty, it's very healthy. But be warned, it'll blow your head off!

You will need:

PIZZA BASE

Makes enough dough for 2 thick-base pizzas that are 12–16 inches (30–40 cm) in diameter.

3¼ cups (410 g) all-purpose (plain) flour

1½ teaspoons active dry yeast

1 tablespoon brown sugar (optional)

1 teaspoon salt

1 cup (250 ml) hot water

TOMATO SAUCE

1 onion, finely chopped

1 garlic clove, crushed

extra-virgin olive oil

1 tablespoon tomato paste

1 can chopped plum tomatoes

1 teaspoon basil, chopped

1 teaspoon oregano, chopped

just under ⅛ cup (8 g) hash, crumbled

salt and freshly ground black pepper

TOPPING

1 cup (225 g) mozzarella cheese

1 cup (175 g) spicy sausage or a handful of anchovies

1. Preheat the oven to 400°F (200°C/gas 6).

2. Mix together all the dry ingredients for the pizza bases first, and then add the water. Work the dough until smooth.

3. Let the dough rise (leave it for approximately 1 hour). Then flatten it out into 2 circular pizza bases.

4. Fry the onion and garlic in a little olive oil. Add the tomato paste and canned tomatoes, basil, oregano, and hash.

5. Cook down to a pulp. Season with salt and black pepper to taste.

6. Spread the tomato sauce on the pizza bases. Grate a good helping of mozzarella cheese on top.

7. Add spicy sausage or anchovies (or anything else you like) on top of your pizzas.

8. Bake in the preheated oven for about 20 minutes, or until the bases are crisp.

9. Garnish with extra black pepper. Serve straight away.

Fruited Ganja Chicken Thighs

What's happening, man?" said Ray Palmer, otherwise known as "The Beat Lord," a hip-hop artist and "samurai guru" from Staten Island, New York.

Greeting each other with a hi-5, I said, *"I've brought you some books, Ray, nice editions of T.S. Eliot's The Waste Land and Ash Wednesday."*

As a hip-hop lyricist, Ray had a real appreciation of poets like Eliot, W.B. Yeats, and Louis MacNeice. After he'd paid me for them, he swung open the door of his shabby-looking closet.

"Christ!" I exclaimed, jumping backward. Inside, hanging from a hook, was a human head. *"What you done, killed someone?"* I said.

"Naw, man," he replied. *"This a shrunken head from Nam. My Uncle Tobias gave it me,"* explained Ray. *"He got it in Nam in 1971. Said a local gave it him. Said it was ancient and would save his life one day. It's a good luck charm."*

I looked closer at the gruesome artifact. *"If that brings you luck,"*

I said, *"I'll let you have the next first edition Eliot I find for free."*

"You're on," he said, laughing. *"Hey, come on, I've got some chicken on the go. Calm your nerves. Dropped a bag of weed in the pot."*

The meal was delicious and I was soon feeling relaxed and centered again. I asked Ray for the recipe and hastily scribbled it down. Here it is:

You will need:

Serves 2–3

6 tablespoons olive oil

1 medium onion, chopped

¼ cup (25 g) celery, finely chopped

1 garlic clove, crushed

2 medium apples, cored and roughly chopped

¼ cup (35 g) raisins

¼ cup (25 g) chopped walnuts

1 egg, beaten

8 large chicken thighs

1 teaspoon dried tarragon

1 cup (60 g) marijuana, finely chopped

1. Preheat the oven to 350°F (180°C/gas 4).

2. In a medium-size skillet (frying pan), heat 2 tablespoons of oil. Add the onion, celery, and garlic. Sauté for about 3 minutes, until the onion and celery are tender. Remove from the heat and add the apple, raisins, walnuts, and egg. Mix well.

3. Prepare the chicken thighs by pulling the skin away from the meat, without removing it. Stuff the apple mixture between the skin and meat.

4. Arrange the chicken pieces in a foil-lined 13 x 9 x 2-inch (30 x 20 x 5-cm) baking dish. In a small bowl, combine the remaining 4 tablespoons of olive oil with the tarragon and marijuana and mix together. Brush this over the chicken thighs. Bake the chicken, uncovered, basting every 15 minutes for 1 hour, until the thighs are tender.

REFRESHMENTS

Turkish Deelight

With all this talk about food, I'm getting thirsty. It must be time for a weed-laced coffee. In fact, it was the Reverend Gary Fox, a DJ and blues guitar player from Texas, who turned me on in a big way to the joys of dope-laced drinks.

I first met him during a U.S. tour I did with my 1990s band, Wildcat Bones. We were supporting his outfit. A blues guitar player myself, I used to stand in awe as this 60-year-old black guy pumped out slick licks to a lively crowd. At the end of one gig, we were holed up in a run-down, backstreet bar in Atlanta, Georgia.

The Reverend Fox says to me: *"Dumb ass kids today like their crack cocaine and meth. Not me. I like to mellow out with a Turkish Deelight,"* he said.

"Tell me, Reverend," I asked, *"what's a Turkish Deelight?"*

"Gonna order you one right now, from the bar," he said. He called over to a young Latino woman behind the bar. *"Hey Angel,"* he says. *"Fuel us up with a couple of Turkish Deelights."*

"It aint legal," the Rev Fox said. *"But they cool around here."*

Ten minutes later, Angel brings over two jet-black coffees.

"Man," I said. *"I've never tasted any coffee as good as this before."*

"You wait, brother," he replied. *"Half-hour from now you'll be on Mars."*

AND I WAS...

If you fancy going orbital, why not try some Turkish Deelight yourself?

You will need:

1 heaped teaspoon finely powdered Arabian mocha

small pinch powdered cardamom seed

½ g pulverized hashish

1 pot good-quality coffee

1 teaspoon honey

1. Place the mocha, cardamom, and hashish in a Turkish coffee pot. Pour on the coffee. Heat the Turkish pot over a low heat until it begins to bubble. Take it off the heat immediately.

2. Serve in espresso cups with a small spoon. Dissolve in the honey. Sip the coffee, and then scoop up whatever is left with the spoon.

Bhang

During the sixties, Aunt Mary Jane, in common with many other dope heads, made a pilgrimage to India. While there, she also studied yoga and meditation, and made the acquaintance of a holy man named Varanasi.

While teaching her the pranayama breathing/meditation method one day, Varanasi said: "Although holy men don't recommend it, you can bypass years of meditation by drinking Bhang. It takes you to the celestial realms and provides a glimpse of enlightenment. But you won't ever achieve true enlightenment if you only take Bhang and give up your meditation."

"Could I try some of this Bhang?" *Mary Jane asked.*

"Of course," *said Varanasi,* "and I'll show you how to prepare it."

Bhang is the name given in India to a drink that contains cannabis. It is legal in many parts of India and is mainly used for spiritual purposes. Rajasthan has licensed Bhang shops and you can buy Bhang products and drinks in many establishments there.

On her return to the U.S., Mary Jane created her own variation of the Bhang drink recipe given to her by Varanasi.

You will need:

1 oz (25 g) marijuana

2 cups (475 ml) boiling water

4 cups (950 ml) warm milk

2 tablespoons blanched and chopped almonds

⅛ teaspoon garam masala (mixture of cloves, cinnamon, and cardamom, available at food stores)

¼ teaspoon powdered ginger

½–1 teaspoon rosewater

1 cup (225 g) sugar

1. Remove any seeds or twigs from the marijuana, and place the leaves and flowers in a teapot. Pour on the boiling water. Put the teapot lid on and let the infusion brew for about 10 minutes.

2. Strain the marijuana water through a tea strainer or cheesecloth, and put the water to one side.

3. Take the leaves and flowers left in the strainer and squeeze out any excess water into the marijuana water.

4. Place the leaves and flowers in a mortar and add 2 teaspoons of warm milk. Using a pestle, slowly and firmly grind the milk and leaves together.

5. Gather up the leaves and flowers and squeeze out as much milk as you can into a bowl. Repeat this process until you have used about ½ cup (120 ml) of milk.

6. By this stage the marijuana should have turned into a pulp.

7. Add the chopped almonds and some more warm milk to the marijuana pulp. Grind this in the mortar until it becomes a sticky paste. Squeeze the paste and collect the extract as before in a bowl. Repeat a few more times until all that is left are some fibers and nut meal. Throw away what's left.

8. Combine all the liquids that have been collected, including the water the marijuana was brewed in. Add the garam masala, dried ginger, and rosewater to the mix. Then add the sugar and remaining milk.

9. Chill in the refrigerator for a few hours. Serve cool and hit the stars!

Green Dragon

Aunt Mary loved to lace fruit juices and sodas with cannabis. She taught me how to extract the THC from marijuana, which allows you to add it to any drink.

THC isn't a water-soluble compound, so you have to extract it using alcohol. In common with fellow dope-heads, Mary Jane called the resulting solution "Green Dragon."

This is what you do:

1. Look out for a bottle of natural-grain alcohol. It's hard to find, so grab more than one bottle if you find some. Use the highest-proof alcohol you can find (if you can get it, 190-proof is highly recommended).

2. Score the best dope you can find. Use about ½ gram of dope per 1 fluid ounce (30 ml) of alcohol.

3. Break up the marijuana and take out the seeds. You can also use the stems.

4. Crack open the bottle of alcohol and pour about a fourth of it away, so there's room for the weed. Carefully add the broken-up dope plant into the bottle. Put the cap back on the bottle and shake.

5. Store the bottle in a safe place (away from sunlight) and let it work its magic for two to three weeks. As time progresses, you'll find the solution begins to take on a green tint (hence the name "Green Dragon").

6. After the two or three weeks are up, pour the green tinted mixture into another container through a strainer, such as a coffee filter or cheesecloth.

7. The result is a high-proof alcohol-laced solution with large amounts of pure THC.

GREEN DRAGON SERVING SUGGESTION

Mix 3 parts of 7-Up or Coke with 1 part Green Dragon. Stir in a spoonful of honey. Serve with ice.

Do the Hashy Hashy (Milk) Shake

A killer way to take your daily dose of hash is with a Green Dragon milkshake. All you need is a food blender. It gives your morning a real buzz.

You will need:

4 ripe bananas

a handful of strawberries

a sprinkle of hash

a sprinkle of honey

2½ cups (600 ml) milk

carton of cream

½ cup (120 ml) Green Dragon

1. Throw the bananas and strawberries into a blender. Sprinkle in some hash and honey.

2. Whiz everything to a pulp.

3. Add the milk, cream, and Green Dragon. Blend again until the whole thing is bubbling. Put into the refrigerator for an hour, and serve cool.

Sundown Cocktail

People are always surprised when I tell them that
I don't drink beer. As I always say, "Beer's way too
strong for me." What I drink is spirits, mostly rum,
bourbon, and vodka. They go down very easily, and I
find they mix well with weed. I know a lot of people
say booze and dope don't mix. I admit, they certainly
don't for a lot of people, but I've never had a problem
with it. Yeah, it's a different buzz to straight dope,
but it'll get you into a mellow burn
as the sun begins to set toward
the end of the day.

This is what you do:

1. Get a tall glass. Fill it a quarter full with Green Dragon. Top it up to half with rum. Then hit the brim with a mix of freshly squeezed orange juice and pomegranate juice.

2. Now, if you're anything like me you won't own a cocktail shaker, so just use a regular bottle and shake vigorously.

3. Drop in some ice for that finishing touch. There's nothing better than sitting down to one of these on a sandy beach under the dying embers of a setting sun.

Flowing with the Tao

Not long after Mary Jane passed, I was listening to the Wu Tang Clan, one of the most artistic and influential U.S. hip-hop acts there has ever been. The leader or "abbot" of the nine-strong outfit, RZA (pronounced "Rizza"), was rapping on one of the tracks about his sorrow at the passing of one of their band members, Ol Dirty Bastard (1968–2004). Ol Dirty Bastard's name, by the way, came from the 1980 Kung Fu film, *Ol' Dirty & The Bastard*.

Most of the members of the Wu Tang Clan are into Kung Fu movies, but RZA is also an expert on Chinese Taoist philosophy and practices Kung Fu, which can best be described as the "moving form" of Taoism.

When his friend Ol Dirty Bastard died of an accidental cocaine overdose, RZA sought solace in Kung Fu and the eternal Tao. It was his way of making sense of it.

And this is the way I also chose to mourn the death of my Mary Jane. My long-time mentor had finally left this earth to walk the pathways of eternity. Like RZA, I turned to the Tao and found a verse from the R.L. Wing translation of the *Tao Te Ching*, which goes:

"Those skillful in the ancient Tao are subtly ingenious and profoundly intuitive. They are so deep they cannot be recognized. Since, indeed, they cannot be recognized, their force can be contained."

I realized just how well that this verse summed up my Aunt Mary Jane's personality. She instinctively followed the Tao and could never be recognized, and her inner power was always contained, never dissipated.

With that, I drank a cup of Turkish Deelight and drove down to the Pacific coast in my black 1968 Ford Mercury to quietly remember the passing of a truly remarkable woman.